KNIGHTS VS SAMURAI

KNIGHTS VS SAMURAI

DOVERPICTURA

DOVER PUBLICATIONS, INC. | Mineola, New York

By Alan Weller

Knights vs. Samurai is a new work, first published by Dover Publications, Inc., in 2011.

Images 118, 147, and 225 were originally rendered by A.G. Smith.

For permission to use more than ten images, please contact:
Permissions Department
Dover Publications, Inc.
31 East 2nd Street
Mineola, NY 11501
rights@doverpublications.com

The CD-ROM file names correspond to the images in the book. All of the artwork stored on the CD-ROM can be imported directly into a wide range of design and word-processing programs on either Windows or Macintosh platforms. No further installation is necessary.

ISBN 10: 0-486-99032-X
ISBN 13: 978-0-486-99032-3

Manufactured in the United States by Courier Corporation
99032X01
www.doverpublications.com

014

015 background

021

022

027

028

16

031   032 background

033 034 19

035

036 background

038

039

040 background

041

042

043

044

045

046

047

048 background

049

050

051

052

25

055

056

058

061

高野
玉川

062

063

065

066

067

068

071

073

074

075

076

077 background

079

080

085

087

088

089

090 background

091

092

093 background

094

095

096

097

098

099 background

101

102

103

54

105

106

113

115

116

64   119   120   121 background

124

125

東都
名所

すだみ
渡し

廣重画

つだ山

127 background   128

129

69

133

135

136

73

140

141 background

142

143

145

146

147 background

149

82   150

151

152

154

155

156

157 background

159

160

162

163

166

167 background

168

169

170 background

171

172

173

174

177

178 background

179

180

99

184   185 background

186

189

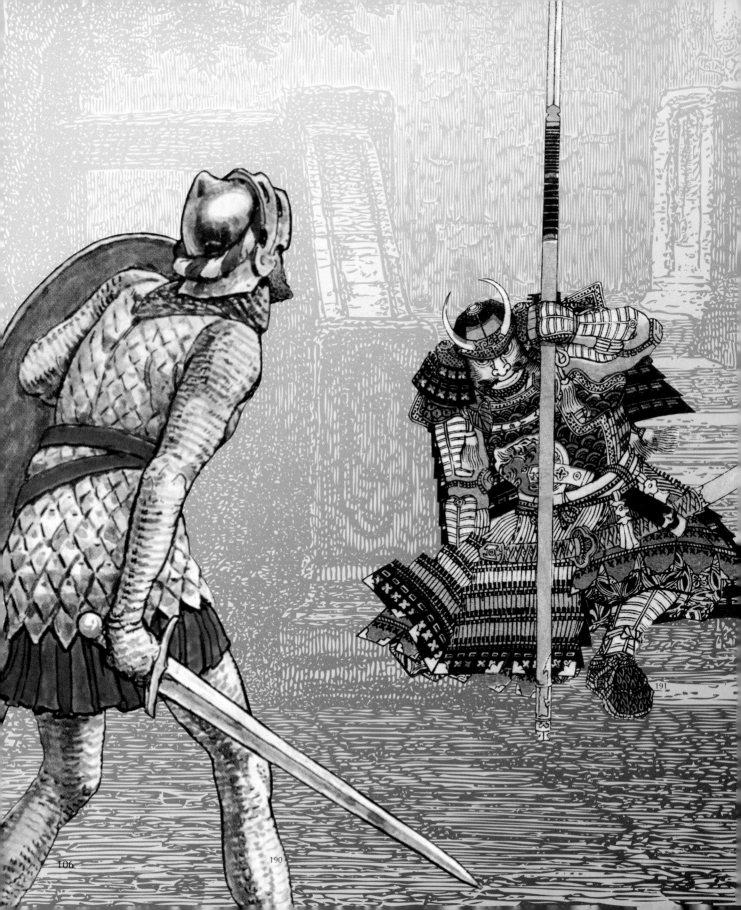

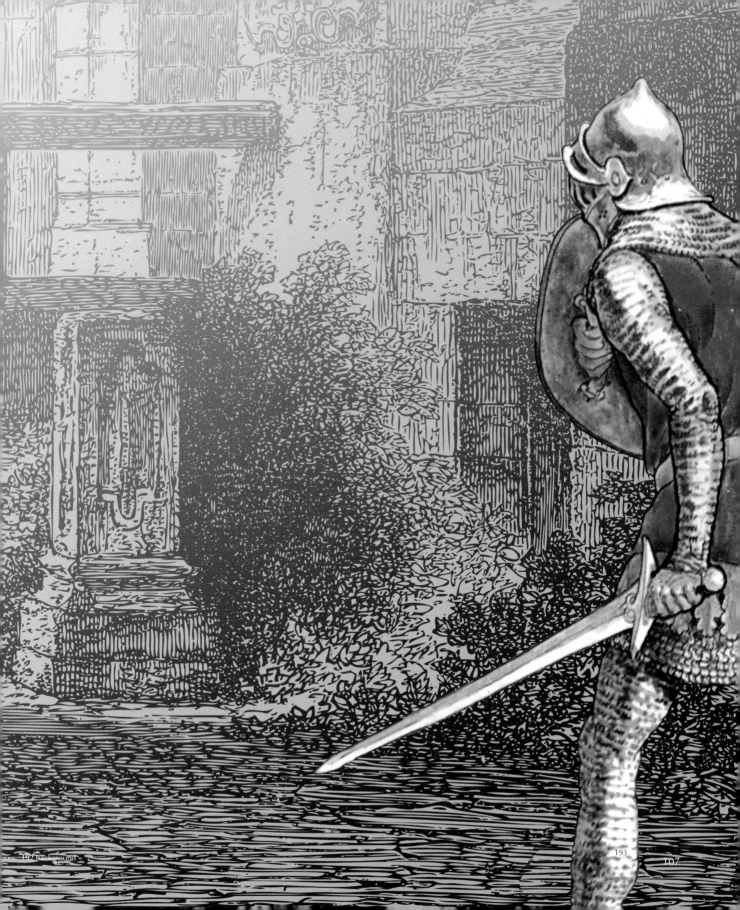

194

197

198 background

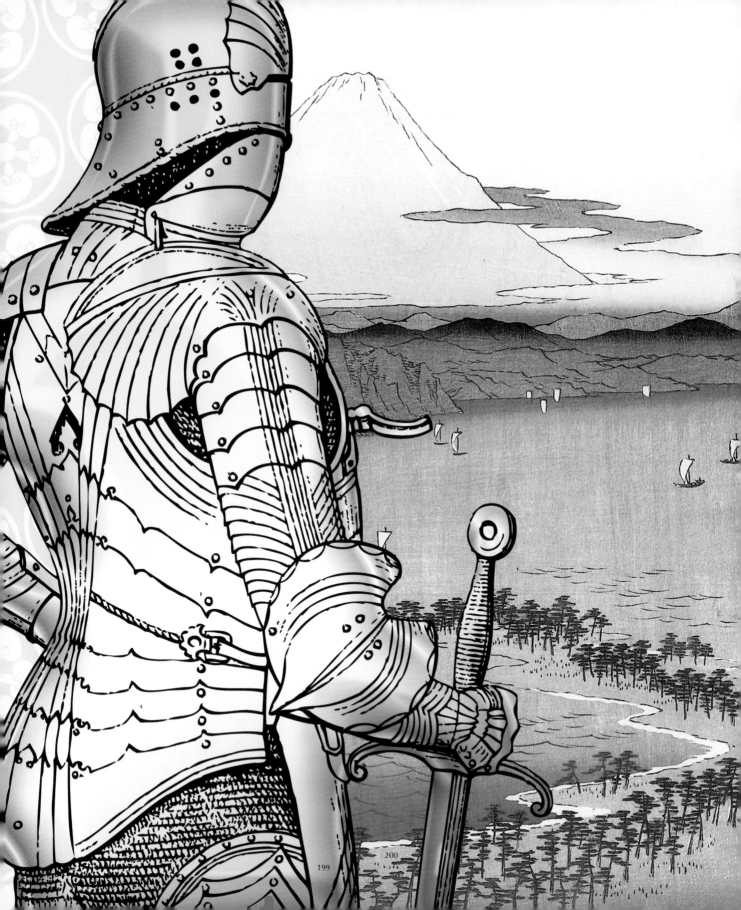

201

202 background

204

205

206

207

208

217

216

215

214

213

212

209   210   211   115

224

225 background

226

230

231 background

232

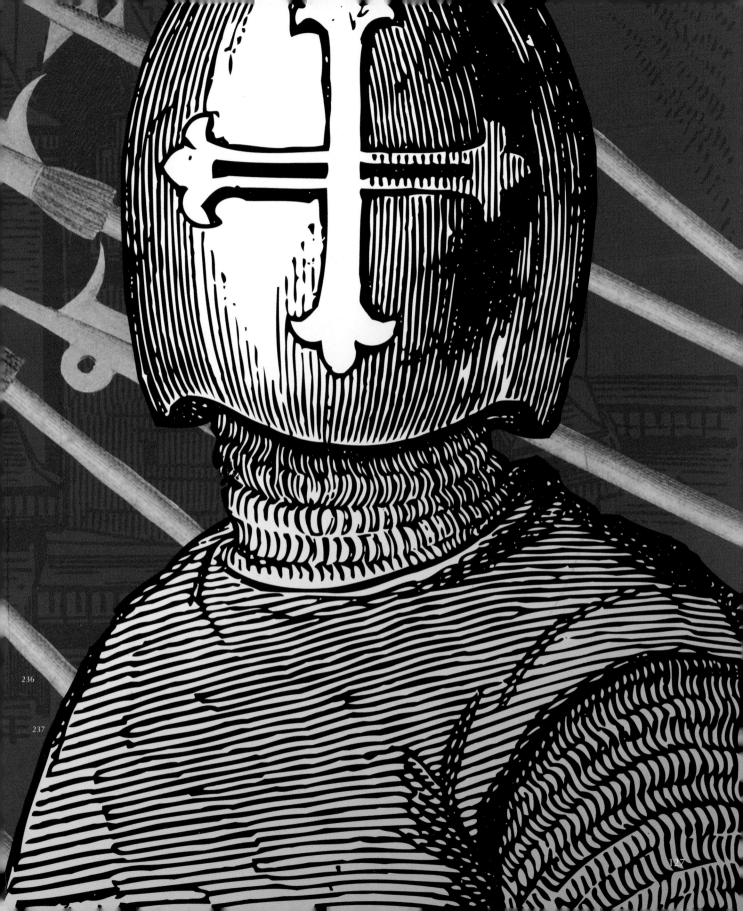

List of Vector Images